Wedding Speeches

Other Titles in:- 'The Wedding Collection'

Wedding Speeches

by: Lee Jarvis

foulsham
LONDON • NEW YORK • TORONTO • SYDNEY

foulsham

The Publishing House, Bennetts Close,
Cippenham, Berkshire, SL1 5AP

ISBN 0-572-01781-2

Phototypeset in Great Britain by:
Typesetting Solutions, Slough, Berks.
Printed in Great Britain by:
St Edmundsbury Press Ltd,
Bury St Edmunds, Suffolk.

CONTENTS

INTRODUCTION

There is to be a wedding. It may be a small wedding or it may be a grand wedding. You are the bride or the groom or the bride's father or the best man. You have to, or wish to, make a speech.

'No problem at all,' you think, when the date is way in the future. 'I've never had to make a speech before, but I'll be among friends. A couple of drinks inside me and I'll put Mark Antony and Abraham Lincoln to shame!'

Then the big day gets closer, and closer, and your self-confidence starts to wane a little. Before you know it, you have those twinges in the stomach that usually go with job interviews, and a huge panic of 'What on earth can I say?' 'Will I make a fool of myself?' 'Will I ruin the whole occasion?'

◊ ◊ ◊

This book won't prevent the stomach twinges — even the most experienced public speakers get them — but, provided you don't postpone reading through it until the last moment, it will stop the panic and should boost your self-confidence. From it you can get ideas for your own speech, or even a ready-made speech that you can adapt as your own. You can find guidance in planning what you are going to say, on preparing yourself and, perhaps most important of all, on how to present your speech.

The Wedding Reception

In this book a traditional English wedding reception is assumed. This may be formal or relaxed, with many guests or just a few.

◇ ◇ ◇

At the reception, the bride's parents receive the guests, who then congratulate the bride and groom and inspect the wedding gifts, if they are on display.

If a formal meal is eaten, the bride and groom sit near the centre of the top table, the bride on her husband's left. On her left sits her father; on his left her mother-in-law. On the bridegroom's right sits his mother-in-law; on her right his father; then, usually, the chief bridesmaid or matron of honour and the best man.

The cake is customarily placed on the top table, but until the moment of cutting it should not be directly in front of the newlyweds. For if it is a tall cake it could obscure them from the sight of some guests.

The toasts come after the meal. It is important to see that everyone has a charged glass when they are made. There is nothing worse than seeing a guest raise an empty glass, and *mime* drinking a health.

The wedding cake is cut by the bride, with the help of her husband, and every guest should eat some of it. Normally the cake is cut after the toasts.

◊   ◊   ◊

All the speeches at wedding receptions are really toasts, and replies to toasts.

The first, to the health of the bride and bride-groom, is normally made by the bride's father. When this is not possible, as for example where the bride's mother is a widow, the speech is made by an old friend of the family. The bridegroom responds for himself and his new wife, and then proposes the second toast, to the bridesmaids or matron of honour.

The reply to this toast is made, not by one of the bridesmaids, but by the best man on their behalf.

At most formal weddings, no other speeches are made, but at less formal receptions, the bride herself may wish to say a few words.

The main thing to remember about a speech at a wedding reception is that it should be brief, ideally not lasting for more than four or five minutes at the very outside. And the best speeches are often shorter still.

Specimen Speeches

Toast to the Bride and Groom

This is normally proposed by the bride's father. If the bride's mother is a widow, the toast should be made by a relative of mature years (an uncle, for example) or an old family friend.

The speech should be quite brief. About three minutes is adequate; five minutes is plenty; more than five minutes is too long.

SPECIMEN 1

'Ladies and Gentlemen — Welcome to you all. I see a lot of happy, smiling faces around me today, but no one looks quite as happy as the two young people on my right.

'Just look at their faces! They say marriages are made in heaven, and while this may be true, this marriage had its origins in my drawing-room, eighteen months ago. Then I introduced Robert to Jean.

'I remember I was helping my wife to do the washing up afterwards — that's a pleasure you have to look forward to, Robert. She said, "I think Jean's taken a fancy to that young man." I paid no attention, of course, but when, six months later, Robert asked my advice about engagement rings, I had to admit she was right.

'When your daughter gets married and leaves home they say, to cheer you up, "You're not losing a daughter, you're gaining a son." In my case I'm also gaining a telephone.

'But if I may be serious for a moment, I could hardly wish for a better son-in-law than this young man. He's a handsome chap, you'll agree, and I know he will make Jean the perfect husband. No, not too perfect, I hope. That would be a little dull, and married life ought to be exciting, a sort of adventure. I know mine has been.

'As for Jean, well, she's a bit of a bargain if I may say so. Though I won't say she's entirely without faults. (I'll have a word about those in private, Robert, if you like, a little later).

'I know, and you know, that these young people are going to be blissfully happy.

'Let us stand then and raise our glasses to them, and make them this wish in the words of the fairy tale. *(Pause)*. To Jean and Robert, may you live happily ever after.'

SPECIMEN 2

'Friends — I know you all too well to address you as Ladies and Gentlemen — I read in a newspaper the other day that marriage was going out of fashion. Of course, you can't believe all you read in the newspapers. But if they were right — well, did you ever see two young people so delighted to be out of fashion?

'Brides are supposed to look radiant, and bridegrooms are supposed to look clean. Well, Karen is certainly the most shining bride I've ever seen. You almost have to shield your eyes to look at her. And Damien *does* look clean. He looks as if he's been scrubbed behind the ears with a hard brush. Perhaps he has — I know they had some pretty useful gifts from all of you!

'I must say Damien has found himself a fine girl in Karen even though she is my own daughter. My wife, who has been a wonderful second mother to Karen, agrees with me. Indeed as we came out of church she turned to me and said, "She'll make something of him."

'There you are Damien, you are warned. You are going to be made something of. This is something that happens to every married man; he is always in danger of being made something of.

'Usually the process is a success. Just look at me, standing here in all my glory. You don't suppose I became the splendid figure I am today by my own efforts? No, I was made something of.

'Now, may I be perfectly serious, as I thank you all for sharing this day with us, and ask you to stand and raise your glasses to the bride and groom. To the luckiest man in England, and his beautiful wife. *(Pause).* Ladies and Gentlemen — To Karen and Damien.'

SPECIMEN 3

'Ladies and Gentlemen — Will you please stand and raise your glasses, to drink with me a toast of long life, good health and happiness to Laura and Simon. Long may they keep open house to three of the best friends they'll ever have — Love, Life and Laughter! To Laura and Simon. *(Pause)*.

'Today is Laura and Simon's celebration. Today they are royalty. King and Queen for the day. I'm merely the humble peasant that foots the bill. Not so much a bill, more like the national debt! Now the humble peasant has to make a short speech saying how much he's enjoying it! It's a very short speech, I've had my orders! From the Queen Mother!

'Mum and I are delighted to welcome you all as our guests. Especially Simon's mother and father, as well as those who have travelled a long way to be here. Thank you for honouring us with your company. And, of course, we remember, with love, those not able to be with us today. *(Slight pause)*.

'We are delighted to see Laura looking so happy and beautiful as she begins her new life with Simon. It's good to have another man in the family, especially someone who will look after our daughter so well.

'All the family is proud of Laura and the excellent match she has found in Simon. We have known him for some time now, and have become very fond of him. He's a good 'un.

'When the father of the bride makes this speech, he's supposed to offer advice to the newlyweds about happiness. I did hear of one vicar who used to advise newlyweds to learn to say the six hardest words in the English language — "Please", "Thank you", and "I am sorry". Another says that "give and take" is the secret, which is what two men in a pub said. "That's right, Harry," said Fred. "That's what we do. My wife and me. Give and take. We give and take all the time. I give her everything, and she takes the lot!"

'That was the serious bit! It now only remains for me to say to Laura and Simon, on behalf of us all, God Bless you both, welcome to the circle of married couples, and may good fortune and every blessing follow you as you set out on the great adventure.'

The Bridegroom's Reply

(and Toast to the Bridesmaids/Matron of Honour)

SPECIMEN 1

'Ladies and Gentlemen — I told my new father-in-law a few minutes ago that I felt nervous about making this speech. He said, "Don't be silly. Everyone *expects* a man to make a fool of himself on his wedding day. They'll be disappointed if you don't." And the last thing I want to do today is to disappoint you. I feel so happy that I want everyone else to be happy.

'Let me say too how delighted Jean and I are that you were all able to come to our wedding. Apart from anything else, we would have felt pretty foolish sitting down here behind this enormous cake if there were no one else to eat it! But we do sincerely thank you for coming, and for the beautiful presents you have given us.

'I have a few personal thank you's to make, too. Firstly to Jean's parents for this marvellous reception. And also because they could not have been kinder to me, the man who has stolen their daughter from them. Secondly, to my own parents, for all they have done for me. And thirdly, to my best man. You wouldn't think, to see him sitting there idly supping champagne, that he is one of the world's great organisers. Well, he is, and his organising ability has been of enormous help to me.

'And last, but by no means least, I must thank the bridesmaids. They all looked absolutely splendid, and if anyone could have stolen my new wife's thunder today, it would have been them.

'I ask you then to drink a toast to these delightful young women who supported Jean in her — I was going to say "ordeal" — on her big day. *(Pause)*. Ladies and Gentlemen — The bridesmaids.'

SPECIMEN 2

'Ladies and Gentlemen — We are told that marriage is a lottery. If it is, then I must be the big winner. I really am the luckiest man in the world, to have Karen as my wife and such good friends as you, to come along and share my happiness.

'I have been lucky in other ways too. Lucky in my new parents-in-law. I don't like that phrase "in-law" much. Perhaps I could call them my "extra parents", for no one could have been more kind to me than they have been.

'And no one could be luckier in his best man than I have been — even if he did whisper in my ear just as Karen was coming up the aisle, "I do hope I haven't forgotten the ring."

'Karen has been lucky too — and I don't only mean in getting me for a husband! I mean in the support of Penny, her charming matron of honour. I think we should all raise our glasses to her, not only for all her hard work today, but also for looking so lovely. *(Pause)*. Ladies and Gentlemen — To Penny.'

SPECIMEN 3

'Friends, Ladies and Gentlemen — I woke up this morning and thought, "Bridegrooms are meant to be nervous, but there's nothing wrong with me." Then I put an entire packet of tea into the teapot, and poured boiling water into the empty tea caddy!

'Those days are over for ever! I am now a married man and life from now on will be much more organised. I see before me an endless stream of clean shirts and darned socks. For that, they tell me, is what married life is all about.

'Seriously, though, I do feel I'm the luckiest man alive to have wooed and won Laura. I like that phrase "wooed and won", it has an old-fashioned air about it. I suppose marriage is an old-fashioned thing to some people, but I have a feeling it will be around for a long, long time. I hope so, anyway. I have been married *(looks at watch)* quite fifty minutes and I have no complaints at all!

'I want to say thank you on behalf of both of us, to all of you for coming to our wedding and for being so very generous in your presents. And I want to say thank you on my own behalf to Laura, for taking me on. To her parents for their tremendous kindness to me. And to my best man, John, who got me to the church on time!

'I have another duty. To propose the health of the bridesmaids and pageboys. This is really more than a duty, it's a positive pleasure. I know the bridesmaids have been very helpful to Laura, not only today, but in those long weeks of preparation that brides go in for. And I know you will want me to thank, also, young Jeremy and Tim, the pageboys, for carrying out their duties so handsomely today.

'Ladies and Gentlemen *(Pause)* the toast is —The bridesmaids and pageboys.'

The Best Man's Reply
(on behalf of the Bridesmaids/Matron of Honour)

SPECIMEN 1

'Ladies and Gentlemen — I am called the best man, but goodness knows why, for no one pays much attention to a man in my position today. They all say, "Isn't the bride radiant?" and "Doesn't the groom look dashing?" and "How pretty the bridesmaids are!" But you never hear anyone say "What a fine figure of a man the best man is!" If they notice me at all they think I'm someone from the caterers.

'But enough of my troubles. I am standing up at this moment to speak for the bridesmaids, to say thank you on their behalf for the kind things Robert said about them.

'To tell you the truth I don't think he did them justice, but then that's understandable on a day like this. I'm surprised he even *noticed* that they were there at all, the way he's been looking at Jean.

'Never mind, I'm still a bachelor and my judgement is emotionally unclouded, and I think they're the finest looking set of bridesmaids I've ever seen. I can see that you all agree with me, so my job is done.

'On behalf of the bridesmaids, thank you very much indeed.'

SPECIMEN 2

'I feel a little strange replying to the toast to the matron of honour, because, as you can all see, I am not a matron — of honour or otherwise. It is, however, a very pleasant job, because I think we all feel that Damien was absolutely right in saying such nice things about Penny.

'I would like to thank him for saying nice things about me, too, though I must admit I, too, rather deserve them. I mean, where would a bridegroom be without his best man? The friend at hand when panic grips him on the very steps of the church. The reassuring voice in his ear when he is absolutely sure he has forgotten some vital detail in his honeymoon arrangements. The wise counsellor who knows just how everything should be done on the most important day in a man's life. I felt sure Damien had picked me for this important job because he had weighed up my fine qualities and thought me ideal.

'And while we were sitting in church waiting for

Karen to arrive I did ask him to confirm this. Do you know what he said? He said, "Oh well, Eric is on holiday and I thought you might just about manage."

'Never mind, I forgive him. The only thing I find it hard to forgive him for is marrying this beautiful young woman, who must surely have preferred me had she known me a little better — or perhaps less well!

'Seriously, though, let me add my good wishes to this handsome couple, and let me say thank you most sincerely on behalf of the matron of honour.'

SPECIMEN 3

'Ladies and Gentlemen, friends and others. Well, they told me to include everybody!

'It is my great pleasure to be here with you on this occasion to help Laura and Simon celebrate their marriage. However, to be best man is a special honour, and I thank Laura and Simon for that invitation. I know they really wanted somebody rich and famous — so here I am!

'My first job is to reply to the toast to the bridesmaids and pageboys, proposed by the bridegroom. We'll all agree how marvellous they have been and I thank him on their behalf for his gifts.

'I am sure you would also want me to give the happy couple the traditional best man's wish — may all their troubles be little ones, all their hopes big ones, and their happiness absolutely fantastic!

'You will expect me to have a bit of fun at Simon's

expense, but Simon's expenses have been so high I'll pass the hat round later!

'Seriously, one of the duties of the best man is to sing the groom's praises and tell everyone about Simon's good points. The problem is, one, I can't sing, and two, he hasn't got any good points! That is, apart from being generous, kind-hearted, good-natured, handsome, and modest — just like me! Actually Simon's more modest than I am, but then, perhaps he's got a lot more to be modest about!

'Some of you may well wonder how a nice girl like Laura came to marry Simon. When Simon was younger he wasn't much of a hit with girls. So he changed his after-shave, and bought some new Y-fronts. Nothing happened. The next thing was to buy all Claire Rayner's books and read them. The girls just giggled. Then he did a crash course in personal magnetism at the Charm School run by Alf Garnett! Zero. Flop. Zilch. Then he met Laura, the only woman in the world for him. And to his amazement she'd have him!

'All he had to do then was resign from the Ancient and Honourable Guild of Bachelors. And there couldn't be a better reason for resigning than getting married to the lovely Laura. He's a very lucky fellow!

'So, thanks to Laura and Simon's marriage today, we have been privileged to come here and enjoy the celebrations with them. I would now like to offer warm and sincere thanks once more, to all who have helped to make this such a successful and happy occasion. Thank you all very much indeed!'

Additions to the Best Man's Reply

At the end of his speech, it is customary for the best man to read out the names of those who have sent congratulatory telemessages, giving the actual greetings from a selection of these.

If the bride is to make a short speech, he should 'introduce' her, briefly. Something like, 'And now, Ladies and Gentlemen, the bride has a few words to say to you . . .' should be sufficient.

He may then be asked to tell the guests what is going to happen next. (If the bride speaks, he should sit and then rise again to say that the cake will now be cut, or the bride and groom will be leaving at a certain time, or that there will be dancing or a disco, or indeed whatever he is asked to tell the guests).

The Bride's Speech

There is really no need for the bride to say any-thing at all on her wedding day. Wedding eti-quette allows no formal place for a speech from her.

However, the custom is growing for the bride to say just a very few words. The ideal place is immediately after her husband has responded to the toast to the two of them, but if he is proposing the toast to the bridesmaids this is difficult. She may prefer to make the last speech, after the best man's reply.

No one is going to expect oratory from a bride on what is, after all, a day on which she must feel some nervous tension. Therefore, no one minds if she falters a little in her speech, or even sheds a tear or two.

Three or four sentences are quite enough for her to deliver publicly.

SPECIMEN 1

'Ladies and Gentlemen — I do not want to say very much. Just that this is the happiest day of my life. And to thank you all for coming to our wedding and being so generous with your gifts.

'I want to say a very special thank you to Robert's parents, who have already made me feel I am their own daughter. Then, to my own parents for looking after me all my life, and for recognising that Robert was the right man to hand me over to. Thank you.'

SPECIMEN 2

'Friends and family — Thank you all for coming along to our wedding! Thanks for your good wishes and all those lovely gifts.

'Ours is a slightly unusual marriage in that Simon and I are good friends! It's a friendship we intend to keep going now that we're married!

'The last word from me has to be one of appreciation to the best Mum and Dad in the world, who have done so much for me in years gone by. Mum's been very special today! In the best families, mother and daughter are not merely parent and child, but good friends too, and that's how it is with us.

'Which is a good note to end on. I propose we drink a toast to three good friends, "Life, Love and Laughter". May those good friends always be friends to us all. *(Pause).* Here's to Friendship.'

At a Second Marriage

Where the bride or the bridegroom, or both, are marrying for the second time, being widowed or divorced, the speeches are usually somewhat different from those at first weddings.

The toast to the bride and groom may still be given by the bride's father, but this is fairly unusual. He is not, after all, giving his daughter away in marriage this time.

Normally this toast will be made by a male friend, or by the best man, if there is one.

As there is much less formality at a woman's second marriage, and if it is held before the registrar, rather than in church, there is less need for a best man.

There are normally only two speeches: the proposal of the new couple's health, and the bridegroom's response. These speeches will probably not have the same lightness and gaiety as at a first marriage. The tone needs to be a little more serious.

Remember that it is bad form to refer to the earlier marriage.

Here is a typical toast at a second marriage.

'Ladies and Gentlemen — It is a real pleasure to me to propose the health of Peggy and Stephen.

'They are both good friends of mine, and when I learned they were to join their lives together, I could not have been happier. I think all of us in this room must feel the same. They are so eminently suited, if I may use a rather old-fashioned term. I am, in any case, a rather old-fashioned person and the sight of a good marriage puts happiness in my heart.

'Let us raise our glasses then, to two of the nicest people I know. Or perhaps I might now say, one of the nicest couples I know. *(Pause)*. To Peggy and Stephen.'

◊   ◊   ◊

The response should be equally brief and simple.

'Ladies and Gentlemen — It was most kind of you to say such nice things about Peggy — my wife, as I must learn to call her — and myself. We are both touched by the knowledge that we have so many good friends who have come here today to wish us well.

'We hope to welcome all of you in our new home when we have settled down.

'I would like to thank you all for your fine gifts, which we appreciate very much. And I would like to express my special gratitude to Marion, who helped Peggy so much with the wedding arrangements, and to Peter, who sorted out one or two tangles for me.

'On behalf of my wife and myself then, thank you.'

Special Situations

Toast to the Bride and Groom (Bride's father deceased)

SPECIMEN

'Ladies and Gentlemen — I feel such pride that I was asked, not only to give the bride away, but also to propose the toast to the happy couple.

'As most of you know, I am Sharon's uncle. Sharon's mother, Maureen, is my big sister —but, looking at our relative proportions, it would be better if I described her as my slim, slightly-older-than-me sister. Sharon's late father, Stan, was my idol. Not only was he the kindest man I've ever known, he was a skilled footballer, a superb 'boogie-woogie' pianist *and* he could charm the hind legs off a donkey with one smile. He would have been so proud of his daughter on this, her special day.

'Sharon has that same smile. I don't know how she fares with donkeys, but she certainly charms every human she meets — especially her husband for the past three hours, Kevin. I first met Kevin when he and Alec — who is best man today — were lodgers in Maureen's home. They were students — of the constantly broke and slightly long-haired variety. I remember that Sharon and Kevin used to bicker and quarrel all the time. Then, suddenly, they fell in love.

'Now, Kevin and Alec are prosperous Accountants — well, they are Accountants and they will start to become prosperous any day now, they assure me. Sharon and Kevin have their own lovely home. And Maureen is with them — very content in the 'Granny Annexe' or 'Maureen's Villa' as Kevin calls it!

'May they all live happily ever after! I'm sure all you good people, whom Maureen, Sharon and Kevin have been so pleased to welcome here, today, will echo that wish.

'So, Ladies and Gentlemen, may I ask you to stand and raise your glasses, to join me in a toast to the bride and groom. *(Pause)*. Sharon and Kevin, may you prosper and live long. And may you always be as happy, healthy and wise as you are today. To Sharon and Kevin.'

Toast to the Bride and Groom
(Bride's father present, but unable to speak)

SPECIMEN

'Ladies and Gentlemen, Friends — Are you all sitting comfortably? Good. Then, to use another familiar catchphrase, "Listen carefully! I shall say this only once!"

'I am honoured to have been asked to help to propose the toast to the bride and bridegroom. As you know, my dear friend, Ted, whom I've always known as Dusty (but who was christened Edwin) has been rather poorly of late. But, with God's help, he recovered so well that he did exactly what he'd always planned to do. He gave his dear daughter Rebecca in marriage to this handsome chap here, Francis.

'Now, I do realise that most of you know the bride as Becky and the groom as Frank. But they have decided, largely because their parents call them Rebecca and Francis, that's how they will be known on this, the most wonderful day in their lives.

'I've known Rebecca since she was a small girl. Even then, she knew she was going to be a nurse. And we all knew too! Everyone calling on Ted and Nora was treated to a good bandaging — that is, if they were lucky! I seemed to spend a great deal of time being sat on a bed pan! So did the dog!

'Then she met Francis. And he was a nurse, too! I remember Ted saying to me, "He's a really nice chap, but I do wish he wasn't a nurse." "Why?" I asked. "A lot of men are nurses. They make good nurses." "Oh, it's not that," said Ted. "It's just that there are two of them practising on me now!"

'Seriously, though, Ted and Nora have asked me to make sure I thank you all, on their behalf, for being here today. They particularly want to thank Francis's parents, Betty and Fred, from the bottom of their hearts, for all the help and support they have given.

'I think that all I have to do now is to wish this radiant young couple, the bride and groom, all the luck in the world, and good health and happiness always. Ted will now propose the toast, so will you all please stand and raise your glasses. *(Pause. Bride's father proposes toast)*. Good luck, good health and happiness, always! To Rebecca and Francis.'

What should You Say?

As with every properly constructed speech, a wedding speech, although brief, must have a beginning, a middle and an end.

When it comes to the serious content of your speech, it is most important to remember that you are proposing or replying to a toast, or both. Some speakers have been so carried away by their flights of oratory that they have sat down without performing this basic duty — to say the only thing they really have to say.

It is quite simple. If you are proposing the toast you simply say at the end of your speech: 'I ask you to rise and drink a toast to ... ' or some such words.

If you are replying the words need not be quite so formal, but you must make it perfectly clear in your speech that you are thanking the company for the toast.

A simple 'thank you very much' is often surprisingly effective. Other formulae you might use are 'I (or we) thank you most sincerely for your kind wishes . . .' 'It was most kind of you to drink to our health and happiness . . .' and so on.

When it comes to rounding off your speech of response, it is quite acceptable to repeat your thanks for the toast, thus avoiding any need to think up a clever ending.

To sum up then: your wedding speech should be brief, but, nevertheless, it must do its job of proposing or responding to a toast.

Should You Tell a Joke?

The art of wit cannot be acquired in a few weeks, however hard you practise. Nor will you succeed in sounding witty by either learning or reading someone else's script written specially for the occasion. A natural or professional comedian's success lies in the ability to act, in facial expression and in the confidence that comes with assured popularity. Few ordinary people possess this talent. If you are one of the lucky ones who do, you will be well aware of your ability and will need little help. If you are not, do not even attempt to make a wholly witty speech. The result will be both painful and boring!

However, there is no reason why you should not tell one, suitable, joke. Indeed, this will help to relax both you and your audience. Twenty years ago a wedding reception was considered no place for comic stories. But times change, and even at the grandest weddings these days the funny story or amusing quotation is quite acceptable.

What is important is that you must not tell a vulgar joke, not even a vaguely risqué one. Think what a nervous strain the day has been for the bride and groom, and reflect how an unsavoury story could embarrass them on this very public and important occasion.

In the same way you must never embarrass the newly-weds with references to their honey-moon, to any previous marriages or liaisons, to the family they may or may not have in the future, or to sex in any form that might offend. However funny your anecdote or joke may be, this is most definitely neither the time nor the place to tell it.

What you can do to raise a laugh is to make fun of yourself, of your shyness, of your inadequacy as a public speaker, of the fact that at least twenty other people could do the job better than you. But you must not make fun of the bride or groom, or any other guest except the best man, who is fair game for a little gentle raillery so long as there is obviously nothing vicious behind your words.

Jokes

Some people are naturally good joke-tellers. If you are in this group you will, no doubt, have noted down a selection of particularly apt jokes from which you can choose. Do remember, though, that anything 'blue' or in any way dubious or offensive is definitely out.

If you are not too good at telling jokes, taking an elaborate joke from a book would probably be a big mistake. The chances are that you would forget the punchline or not tell it well enough to make the wedding guests laugh. Nothing falls flatter than a joke which no one understands or thinks funny.

Find, instead, a short, simple joke that will make your audience smile rather than howl with mirth, and which will fit the situation. Look through the jokes in Chapter Five; hopefully you will see one that appeals to you — perhaps after some slight modification.

Funny stories or anecdotes can often be more easily fitted into a speech than jokes. Some appropriate examples are given in Chapter Six. You might find one of these useful.

Do choose a joke or anecdote that will fit into your speech quite naturally. If you slot one in just for its own sake it will sound out of place.

Few of us can be sure just what others will find amusing so, when you have selected a joke or anecdote, try it out on friends or family. Judge by their reactions whether or not you have made a good choice.

Preparing Your Speech

Getting Started

Above all, start early! Get as many facts and details as you can. What kind of wedding is it to be? Here, we assume a typical English wedding. Other weddings — for example, Jewish, Irish, Scottish, Caribbean, Asian, or inter-faith — will, or may, follow a different pattern.

Make sure you know the type of reception that is being planned and which speechmaker will be responsible for saying what. A speech that is perfect for a formal occasion, with a hundred or so guests, may well sound out of place at a small reception, with only a handful of friends and relations present.

◊   ◊   ◊

If you are the best man, check that there *will be* bridesmaids, that they *will* be presented with gifts, and that *you* are to reply on their behalf. Discovering 'on the day' that half of your speech is useless — or has already been made by a previous speaker — will do nothing for your self-confidence.

Try to find out if there are sensitive areas of which you should be wary, such as family feuds and rivalries, or broken marriages, and ask to be kept informed about family bereavements or serious illnesses that might temper the tone of your speech. And, of course, if you are proposing the health of the bride and groom, don't mention the bride leaving home if she and the groom have been cohabiting in unwedded bliss. That could cause embarrassment.

In fact, make your aim that no one will be, in any way, embarrassed, hurt, offended or bored by anything you say. Then you will be in the right frame of mind to come up with a good speech.

Your Speech

Using a Specimen Speech

By far the simplest way to prepare your speech is to take one of the Specimen Speeches in Chapter Two — the one that best seems to fit the occasion — and change the names and facts to suit. You can take out the sentences that don't apply, and add sentences that do, but do try to maintain a 'flow' of ideas.

Writing your own Speech

If you prefer not to 'lift' a speech, you could work on developing one of them with your own, or different, material. You could include a joke or a quotation — some examples are given in Chapter Five — but do avoid anything that would be more appropriate at the groom's stag party! You may well get a laugh from some of the guests, but you could spoil the bride's day. And the golden rule is, one joke, or at most two, and keep it/them short.

◊   ◊   ◊

The other alternative is for you to write your own speech from 'scratch'. If you are choosing this way, do remember the obvious! Any speech should have a beginning, a middle and an end. Anything less than two minutes (between 200 and 250 words) may seem a little short, but provided everything you want to say is included, it will be sufficient. Anything longer than ten minutes and you risk boring the guests to distraction.

Always remember that you are 'writing for speaking', not 'writing for reading'. Don't make life difficult for yourself by including words that you could stumble over or sentences so long that they'll have you gasping for breath and your audience bewildered as it tries to follow you (as, for example, if you used a sentence such as *this* one in your speech!).

The first step, then, is to list — as headings if you like — all the points you wish to make in your speech. The groom's list, for example, could be: Thank George and Margaret for the reception/ Thank George for his welcome into family and for his toast/Thank my mother and father for all they've done for me/Thank Tom for being best man (make a joke?)/Say how Jenny and I met and how lovely she looks/Praise the bridesmaids/Toast to bridesmaids.

The next step is to make a draft of the middle and end of your speech, including everything you want to, or have been asked to say and, of course, the toast or reply to a toast, as appropriate. Cross off the headings from your list as you write them into your draft. Make sure what you have written is reasonably to length, and that the two sections are linked, so that your speech will 'flow'.

If your draft seems too long, edit out any repetitions or unnecessary sentences. If it seems too short, look to see where a suitable quotation or joke might fit, or be made to fit, naturally.

That leaves you with the beginning of your speech — and here you have some conventions to fall back on. 'Ladies and Gentlemen' (or 'Ladies, Gentlemen — Friends', if you fear you'll sound like the late Frankie Howerd), starts you off.

If you are proposing the toast to the bride and groom, you may now like to welcome your guests, perhaps mentioning some by name. If you are the groom, you'll be expected to say how nervous you are and how lucky you are, before going on to thank your in-laws. If you are the best man, you can start by thanking the bride and groom for wanting you to be best man, and then go on to praise them. However, if you are still 'stuck' on how to start, the ideas in Chapter Five are yours for the taking.

Once you have completed your draft speech, keep it with you, so that you can look at it from time to time, and change and polish it as you get more information and better ideas. But, do keep the sentences flowing together! A fairly good speech that 'flows' will be much better received than a disjointed speech which is no more than a list of clever ideas.

A Special Word to the Best Man

Never!

1 Mention previous girlfriends or anything the least bit dubious in the groom's past.
2 Mention past marriages or relationships.
3 Speak for longer than four or five minutes.
4 Say, 'Unaccustomed as I am to public speaking'.
5 Use unnecessarily long words or sentences.
6 Use formal words or phrases that you would not normally use.
7 Tell lies.
8 Put on an accent.
9 Be pompous or patronising.
10 Use slang.
11 Tell 'in' jokes which not all the audience will understand.
12 Swear or blaspheme.
13 Tell risqué jokes.
14 Make fun of anyone, in any way unkindly, except yourself.
15 Refer to the honeymoon or future children.

Some Opening Lines, Quotations and Jokes for your Speech

Some Ideas for Opening Lines

'Ladies and Gentlemen — I'm nothing if not original.'

◊   ◊   ◊

'Ladies and Gentlemen — You were expecting that, weren't you?'

◊   ◊   ◊

'Ladies and Gentlemen — I *am* accustomed to public speaking. The problem is, knowing what to say!'

◊   ◊   ◊

'Ladies, Gentlemen, Friends. I am afraid that I am not much of an orator. In fact, I think the last speech I made in public was at my own wedding!'

◊   ◊   ◊

'Ladies and Gentlemen — Who says flattery doesn't work?'

◊   ◊   ◊

'Friends — I wrote my speech down so I remembered to say everything I'm supposed to say. That was alright until this morning, when I found I'd forgotten where I'd put my speech!'

◊   ◊   ◊

'Friends — Welcome to you all. They tell me that marriage is a good thing. I've thought about that a lot. Certainly, if it weren't for marriage, husbands and wives would have to argue with strangers! . . . But seriously, though, . . .'

◊   ◊   ◊

'Ladies and Gentlemen — When you get older, three things start to happen. First, you lose your memory *(pause and look blank)* . . . I can't remember the other two things!'

'Ladies and Gentlemen — I wrote down my speech because my memory isn't all that great. Then I found I couldn't read my own writing! So I had it typed. Now, all I have to do is stop my hands from shaking. Then I might manage to get through it!'

◊   ◊   ◊

'Ladies and Gentlemen — Today is Trish and Philip's big day. The world belongs to them, and we are here to help the celebrations.'

'Ladies and Gentlemen — This is the happiest day of my life, and what is making it so, is the lovely girl sitting next to me.'

'Friends — I'm not going to say very much, except that life is full of surprises. And, for sure, Michael is the best surprise that has ever happened to me.'

'Ladies and Gentlemen — Sally, my wife, and I, want to say a big "Thank you" to you all for joining us on what will probably turn out to be the best day of our lives! . . . or so we've been warned, anyway!'

'Ladies and Gentlemen — Well, as the earwig said when he fell off the tree, 'ere we go!'

Some Appropriate Quotations

If you are including a quotation in your speech, try to lead into it naturally. Introductions such as, 'Nevertheless, as Shakespeare wrote . . .', 'This reminds me of the words of Jonathan Swift (which the librarian looked out for me yesterday) . . .', or 'You all know the old song . . .', are very useful.

'Marriage is a wonderful institution, but who wants to live in an institution?'

Groucho Marx

◊   ◊   ◊

'Marriage is a sort of friendship recognised by the police.'

◊   ◊   ◊

'Marriage is popular because it combines the maximum of temptation with the maximum of opportunity.'

George Bernard Shaw

◊   ◊   ◊

'He's the most married man I ever saw.'

Artemus Ward

◊　◊　◊

'Love makes the world go round.'

Popular Song

◊　◊　◊

'Whatever women do, they must do twice as well as men to be thought half as good. Luckily, this is not difficult.'

Charlotte Whitton

◊　◊　◊

'I have always thought that every woman should marry, and no man.'

Benjamin Disraeli

◊　◊　◊

'A happy bridesmaid makes a happy bride.'

Alfred, Lord Tennyson

◊　◊　◊

'Marriage is an attempt to change a night owl into a homing pigeon.'

◊　◊　◊

'The critical period in matrimony is breakfast time.'

A. P. Herbert

'There's nothing like a wedding,
To make a fellow learn.
At first he thinks she's his'n,
But quickly learns he's her'n.'

'Each man spoils the one he loves,
And gratifies her wishes.
The rich man showers her with gifts;
the poor man dries the dishes.'

'All husbands are alike, but they have different faces so you can tell them apart.'

'Marriage is the alliance of two people, one of whom never remembers birthdays, and the other never forgets them.'

Ogden Nash

'Being a husband is like any other job. It's easier if you like the boss.'

'Your heart's desires be with you.'

William Shakespeare

Some Jokes for your Speech

Again, remember to lead into your joke. An 'old' joke may be better received than a 'new' one. What is important is 'the way you tell it'.

For the Bride's father

'A wife says to her husband, "How would you like to celebrate our silver wedding?" He says, "How about having two minutes' silence?" '

'I think that it's right to warn you that Sally's mother has made the wedding cake, from a powerful recipe she often uses, known to the family as gateau blaster.'

'Jack, be a good lad and avoid argument. If you win you are in dead trouble. Just learn to apologise. That's the best way of getting the last word!'

'Sheila — live within your means. If you can't, live within his. Failing that, borrow. I don't mean come to your father if you are stuck. That's what I did!'

'Les says he's a keen football fan and he's an Arsenal supporter. I've never quite understood the connection!'

'When Norman asked me for Tracy's hand in marriage, I wanted to ask him what was wrong with the rest of her. But I didn't in case he changed his mind! You see, he's actually got a job!'

For the Groom

'A teacher asked her class of six-year-olds, "What is a bridegroom?" They all looked puzzled. Then, one small girl raised her hand. "I think it's a thing they have at weddings," she said hopefully.'

'The brain is a wonderful thing. It never stops working from the time you are born until the moment you start to make a speech.'

'Thanks also to Bill for being best man. Bill is a builder and builders are well-known for getting their days mixed up. I, for one, was relieved when he turned up on the right day. And even more pleased that he remembered it was a wedding, and left his wellies and hard hat at home!'

'This is the second time today that I've risen from a warm seat with a piece of paper in my hand!'

'You can tell from the compliments I'm paying him what good friends Bill and I are. At heart he's a stout fellow. Well, stout, beer, red wine, white wine . . .'

'John and Mary, my in-laws, have been wonderful. John was telling me that while Laura and Mary were going through the wedding arrangements, Laura said, "I'm so afraid we'll overlook some little detail." "Don't worry," said Mary. "I'll see he gets there!" . . . And, as you see, she did!'

For the Best Man

'People keep asking me how old Steve is. There's a simple answer. Old Steve is doing very well!'

'Andy, at work, is incisive and very much in charge. But what do we find here? That this happy couple met eleven years ago, and have been engaged for ten of those years. I ask myself, what was the big rush? Why now?'

'Jack — remember there's no place like home! Well, after the other places close, anyway!'

'Diane is a pillar of the church, busy and active. Jeff is a caterpillar of the church, soft, furry and slow-moving. But, with luck, he'll turn into something beautiful.'

'Simon's piano-playing is really something! It's been heard by people in Australia. They all emigrated when they heard him practising!'

'Caroline and Garry remind me of the story about the princess and the frog! Unfortunately though, no matter how many times she kisses him, he doesn't turn into a prince. Never mind, Caroline. Keep trying!'

Some Appropriate Anecdotes

At some informal wedding receptions, the speechmakers may be expected to come up with a funny story or two to lighten the proceedings. Here are a few ideas.

'The couple had been married for a year. One day she shyly confessed she'd been shopping and had bought ten new dresses. "Ten!" he exploded. "What could any wife want with ten new dresses?" She smiled sweetly at him. "Ten new hats?" she ventured.'

'At the railway station, the new bride turned to her new husband and whispered, "Darling, I don't want the other passengers to guess we're honeymooners. Let's act as if we've been married for years." The groom looked a bit dubious. "But are you *sure* you can manage both suitcases, darling?" he asked.'

'A woman, who was delighted with the effect a patent medicine was having on her, wrote to the manufacturers. "Since taking your tablets I am a different woman," she wrote. "My husband is delighted." '

'A young man was trying to explain the mysteries of the betting shop to his girl friend. "If you back a horse for a pound at five to one and it wins, you get five pounds. If you back it at ten to one, you get ten pounds. And if you back it at twenty to one, you get twenty pounds." "Oh, I see!" she said, thinking deeply. "But what do I get if I back it at exactly one o'clock?" '

'The bride-to-be's father asked his prospective son-in-law, "Well, young man, will you be able to support a family?" "Actually, no, sir," came the answer. "I was only planning to support your daughter. I'm afraid the rest of you will have to look after yourselves." '

'A psychiatrist opened the door to receive his next patient, and saw to his surprise that she was carrying a live duck under her arm. Naturally, being a psychiatrist of some considerable experience, he refrained from any comment. Instead he offered the lady a seat and asked how he could help her.

"Oh no, doctor," she replied, "it's not me who needs help, it's my husband. I've brought him in because he thinks he's a duck." '

'One day, in ancient Rome, the Emperor was entertaining his guests at the Coliseum where Christians were being thrown to the lions.

'He was not amused however, when one of the Christians seemed to whisper in the attacking lion's ear, at which the great roaring beast turned tail and slunk off. The Christian did the same thing as each lion leapt up to him, with the same instant, and astonishing, effect.

'The Emperor was furious, but also intrigued. He had the Christian brought before him and promised to spare his life if he would reveal his secret power over the lions.

' "I have no special magic Your Highness," the Christian replied. "I simply tell them that they will, of course, have to make a speech to the assembled crowd after they have finished their dinner." '

'A diplomat was seated at an important banquet next to an important visitor from China. He realised that it would be rude to say nothing, but what on earth could one say to a Chinese? The soup arrived, and desperately the diplomat smiled and said, "Likee soupee?" The Chinese nodded, and that was the extent of their conversation throughout the meal.

'After the coffee, the visitor was called upon to speak. He rose and made an excellent speech in faultless English, without a trace of an accent. Then he sat down and said to the diplomat, "Likee speechee?" '

'It was a big society wedding and the last speech was delivered by a very distinguished guest, who went on and on and on. Afterwards, he said to the young reporter who was covering the event for the local newspaper, "Please don't quote any of my anecdotes. I'll probably want to use them again next time."

'Anxious to please, the reporter ended his write-up, "The distinguished guest told several stories which, unfortunately, cannot be repeated here." '

'Five-year-old Sharon was sitting thoughtfully between her parents. "Mummy, Daddy," she said. "I *am* glad you named me Sharon." "Why is that, dear?" asked her mother. "Well," said Sharon, "that's what all the children at school call me." '

'A couple were discussing their wedding plans. "Where would you like to go for the honeymoon?" the groom asked. The bride gazed at him adoringly, "Darling, with you I'd go anywhere.

But, since you are asking me, I'd like to go some-where warm, somewhere different and some-where that I've never been before." So he took her into the kitchen.'

'A newly married couple went to Eastbourne for their honeymoon where the hotel was full of rather elderly ladies. When the young couple arrived, the bride, feeling rather nervous and self-conscious, whispered to her husband, "Don't tell them that we're on our honeymoon. I don't want anyone to know we're just married."

'Next morning the young couple came down to breakfast to be greeted by frowns and disap-proving looks. "I wonder why they're all looking at us so disapprovingly," whispered the blushing bride. "Well, you told me you didn't want them to know we're honeymooners," said her husband. "So I told them we're not married." '

Preparing Yourself for your Speech

This chapter is largely addressed to the male speechmakers at a wedding. As long as the bride can be seen and heard by all the guests, and is clear on what she is going to say, no one will mind at all if she fidgets, giggles or sheds a few tears on the groom's shoulder. It is, after all, *her* day.

You, as a male speaker, will be expected to give, at least, a competent *performance*. So, as soon as you have your speech reasonably worked out, take a good look at yourself and decide where there might be room for improvement. Spend a little time ironing out any failings you recognise in yourself, and remember the age-old advice to public speakers — 'Stand up. Speak up. And Shut up.' — and *your* performance will be competent indeed.

How will you present your speech?

You could write it down clearly and read it out. Not the best way by any means. If you keep your head down, to read, you'll probably be indistinct or sound as if you are reading out the company accounts. If you lift your head, your 'script' may obscure your face or you may look as if you are going to burst into song.

An alternative would be for you to learn your speech by heart and then recite it. This would be better than reading it out, but only if you are a capable reciter who won't forget the 'next line'. And, you could have problems with last minute changes to what you have learned!

Sometime when you are alone, try out both ways. Stand in front of a mirror, hold your 'script' as you intend to at the wedding, and read the first few lines out loud — loud enough to be heard at the back of the room or hall where the reception is to be held. Do you sound as if you are announcing the train arriving at Platform One? Now try learning those few lines by heart, then recite them — again to be heard at the back of the reception room or hall. Will you be unnerved staring out at all those guests for several minutes?

By far the best method of presenting your speech is a compromise between reading it and reciting it. For this, you will need to get thoroughly familiar with your speech, learning by heart only the vital facts — particularly names and dates.

On your 'script', mark all the paragraph starts, in red, so that if you lose your place you'll be able to get back on course quickly and painlessly. If it helps you, use a different colour to mark in some 'pauses' — for effect, or where you hope for a laugh from your audience. You might need to take a sip of water on the day, and it could be useful to know where you can manage this without breaking up the flow of your speech.

Next, read through your speech to yourself several times, until you feel it is becoming familiar to you. Then, standing in front of the mirror, try performing your speech, making sure your voice will reach those at the back. Look out as if at the guests most of the time — letting your gaze move about a bit — and down at your written words briefly, as you need to refresh your memory. You should remember that you will be standing and the guests will be seated, so you will need to incline your head downwards, just a little, when addressing them.

Using this method of presentation, you will be able, on the day, to include the occasional *ad lib* should you so wish. This would allow you to bring your speech right up to date, perhaps with a brief mention about the dreadful weather, or the bridegroom turning up late, or whatever.

Irritating habits

Do you have any — particularly when you are nervous? Be very critical of yourself because, for the time it takes you to deliver your speech, you'll have to keep them to a minimum. Do you perhaps run your fingers through your hair, or needlessly realign your glasses? Are you a compulsive ear-lobe puller or nose rubber or finger nail inspector? Most of us have irritating habits so, if you think you are without them, it might be worth checking with a close relative or friend!

No one at the wedding will expect you to stand woodenly when your nose itches, but few will consider you competent if you continually twitch about. So, while you are rehearsing your speech, give some effort to relaxing and to controlling any tendency to fidget. If, on the day, you get an itch, scratch it. But not throughout the whole speech!

Now, return to your mirror. Hold your 'script' as you intend to at the ceremony and stand, looking at yourself. If you have one hand free, will you wave that arm about when you speak? A few natural gestures are fine but too much arm flapping is distracting — and you are liable to demolish a few glasses as you get into 'full flight'. Practise standing with your free arm relaxed at your side, or even loosely in your trousers pocket if it gets 'the shakes'. Then, occasionally lift the arm to turn a page of your script, to indicate, naturally, persons you may be addressing or proposing to toast, to lift your glass for a toast — or for that scratch previously mentioned.

Next, stand as you intend to stand at the ceremony. Do not touch the table in front of you or the chair behind you. Will you wobble or shuffle as you make your speech?

Or, worse still, will you sway to and fro? Try moving your feet a little more apart until you find the position where you feel comfortable and relaxed, with your feet firmly planted and your body — while not still — certainly not emulating a pendulum.

Finally, make sure you can turn a little to your left (or right) without shuffling about and without becoming unbalanced. This is because, at certain points in your speech, you'll want to look towards people to your left or right, for example, towards the bride and groom, the best man or the bridesmaids, as you address or refer to them.

Delivering the words

Being heard

If the reception is to be held in a large room or hall, microphones may well be provided for the speechmakers. In such a case, practise your speech with the aid of the microphone supplied with most tape recorders and cassette players. Listen to what you have recorded, and modulate or modify your speaking technique until you have it to your own satisfaction. Do remember, though, that all microphones are different! And, it's worth finding out if the reception micro-phones are of the hand-held type, or on stands, or clipped to the lapel. If they are hand-held, you will have to rethink what you are going to do with your free hand, as discussed above!

If there are no microphones, you will need to project your voice so that you can be heard by all. But *never* shout. Try speaking slightly more slowly and deliberately than you normally speak, and lower the pitch of your voice just a little. Speak a few lines from your speech out loud, then just a bit louder, then a little louder still if it is to be a large room. After a few runs through, you'll get your level right.

Breath control

One of the hazards of being a first-time public speaker is forgetting to breathe. Practise breath-ing properly and easily as you rehearse your speech. Take in a good breath at the beginning of each sentence. Pause briefly and take in another whenever you need to. Remember, never use up all of your breath before replenishing your lungs; you don't in normal conversation, so don't when speechmaking.

Accents and Pronunciation

It may well be that you have an accent, local or foreign — most people have, to some extent or another. Don't, whatever you do, try to change it. It is part of *you* and *you* are the person making the speech, not an aspiring Newscaster! If your accent is really difficult to follow, just slow down a little, and try to avoid any dialect or foreign words.

But, accent or not, don't be sloppy about pronunciation. Take care with h's and with the words ending in 'd', 't' and '-ing'. You'll probably be easily understood in fast conversation if you say "Th' bri' wen' 'ome wearin' a re' 'a'." But, when spoken slowly in a speech, the guests at the back will have as much difficulty in comprehending it as you have had in deciphering it here!

That's really all there is to it. Keep practising, keep relaxing and you *will* give a very competent performance at the wedding reception — for sure!

On the Day

The Sequence of the Speeches

The speeches and toasts are normally given after the last course when there is a formal sit-down meal, or after the guests have finished eating in the case of a buffet reception. After the speeches the cake can then be cut and coffee served. Since you are making a speech, those responsible for the wedding arrangements will have confirmed with you, exactly what the sequence will be.

Someone will have been appointed toastmaster, to introduce the speakers. At formal weddings with a large number of guests, a professional toastmaster may have been booked. In most cases, though, the task falls to the best man.

At the appropriate moment he will rise, ask for

the attention of the guests and introduce the father of the bride — or whoever is making the opening speech. A simple 'Ladies and Gentlemen — the father of the bride' or 'Ladies and Gentlemen — Mr John Green, the bride's uncle, will now propose a toast to the bride and groom', is all that is needed.

When the toast has been drunk and the guests are once again seated, the best man will rise to introduce the next speaker. 'Ladies and Gentlemen — the Groom' will usually suffice.

He then has to introduce himself — unless the groom has introduced him at the end of his speech, after the toast to the bridesmaids. If he has not been introduced, he should rise and say something like, 'Ladies and Gentlemen — You have probably realised by now that I am the best man'.

At the end of his speech, the best man will probably read out a few telemessages and — if the bride has chosen to speak, next introduce her: '. . . and I'm sure you'll all be delighted to learn that the Bride wishes to say a few words to you . . .

Ladies and Gentlemen — the Bride', would be appropriate.

Finally, he may be asked to announce the cutting of the wedding cake and to tell the guests the programme for the rest of the reception — when the bride and groom will be leaving, if there is dancing, etc.

It may seem that a best man's lot is quite an arduous one! However, they all seem to perform admirably and most even enjoy the experience.

Now, however, let us concentrate on you, as just a speechmaker — with no extra tasks, arduous or otherwise.

Let us assume that everything at the reception is going to plan. If there are microphones, they have been previously tested and you know how to use them. So there will be no need for the dreaded 'Can you hear me at the back?', 'No!', giggle-guffaw routine, which distracts the guests and makes for a nervous first speech-maker.

If there are no microphones, an Usher, or another reliable friend, has been asked to stand near the back of the room to signal if voice levels are about right, or if the speakers should be quieter or louder. The meal has been eaten and the glasses are about to be replenished for the toasts.

So, what have you forgotten to do? ... Quite simply, go to the loo! And, well before the speeches are due to start. It may amuse the guests to see the best man rushing back from the Gents just as the bride's father rises to make his speech, but it won't please those at the top table too much.

Your Speech

The guests' glasses are now filled; the guests are looking expectantly towards the first speaker. There is a babble of conversation from one table. Two small children are noisily disputing the ownership of a spoon. A small baby is crying lustily as he is prodded by a well-meaning aunt. In other words, this is a typical English wedding reception! And, it is where the confident and competent best man comes into his own.

Making sure the speechmakers are there, and

ready, he should rise and smile at the guests in a friendly way, lightly tapping a tumbler for attention. If the noise does not subside, he should again tap the tumbler, pause, and then say very clearly, 'Ladies and Gentlemen, your attention please!' When all is quiet, he should turn towards the first speaker, introduce him to the guests and, with a slight movement of the hand, indicate all is ready for him to rise and begin his speech. Should the children continue to play noisily, the best man may wish to say, as pleasantly as he can, something like: 'Could someone please look after the children while the speeches are being made? . . . Thank you *so* much!'

As you make your speech, do remember to smile. Don't grin inanely but, at least, look happy. Remember your pauses. If something you say causes a laugh or a murmur of conversation, wait for reasonable quiet before proceeding. Never try to shout over the noise.

Remember, for the length of your speech, you are in charge. It sometimes happens that a would-be comedian among the guests interrupts a speech. If what he says is funny, smile, wait for the laughter to subside, and carry on without comment. If he's not funny, wait for him to be quiet, ignore him and again carry on with your speech without comment. If you find you've made a mistake, smile at yourself, say a simple and charming 'Sorry', and correct your error.

◊   ◊   ◊

Before you know it, you'll be proposing the toast or saying your final thank you. It will be all over for you, except for the applause. You were among friends; they wanted you to do well and you have; you've helped in making this a day to remember; you were a competent speechmaker.

◊ ◊ ◊

The *next* time you are called upon to make a speech in public you'll accept with delight, knowing exactly what is involved and feeling supremely self-confident . . . *won't* you??

◊ ◊ ◊

It usually takes me more than three weeks
to prepare a good impromptu speech.
(Mark Twain)

Other Wedding Titles
of Interest

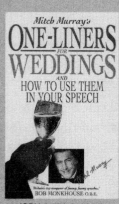

ISBN 0-572-01896-7
£7.99

ISBN 0-572-02338-3
£7.99

ISBN 0-572-02339-1
£3.99

ISBN 0-572-01930-0
£2.99